Short Walks in
The Peak District

Published by Collins
An imprint of HarperCollins Publishers
77-85 Fulham Palace Road,
Hammersmith, London W6 8JB

www.harpercollins.co.uk

Copyright © HarperCollins Publishers Ltd June 2010

Original text © Brian Spencer

Collins® is a registered trademark of
HarperCollins Publishers Limited

Mapping generated from Collins Bartholomew
digital databases on the inner front cover and
all walk planning maps

This product uses map data licensed from
Ordnance Survey ® with the permission of the
Controller of Her Majesty's Stationery Office.
© Crown copyright. Licence number 399302

Printed in China

ISBN   978 0 00 735944 8
Imp 001   XJ12503 / UCD

e-mail: roadcheck@harpercollins.co.uk

Contents

Introduction   4
How to use this book   15
Photo credits   96

▶ Short walks

walk 1: **Derwent Moors**
4¾ miles (7.6km)   16

walk 2: **Combs**
4 miles (6.4km)   20

walk 3: **Peak Forest**
4¼ miles (6.8km)   24

walk 4: **Shatton Moor**
4½ miles (7.2km)   28

walk 5: **Carl Wark & Higger Tor**
3¾ miles (6km)   32

walk 6: **Padley Gorge**
3¾ miles (6km)   36

walk 7: **Birchen Edge**
4 miles (6.4km)   40

walk 8: **Miller's Dale & Wormhill**
5 miles (8km)   44

walk 9: **Solomon's Temple**
4½ miles (7.2km)   48

walk 10: **White Nancy**
4 miles (6.4km)   52

walk 11: **Dovedale**
4½ miles (7.2km)   56

walk 12: **Longnor Two Valleys Walk**
4 miles (6.4km)   60

walk 13: **Elton & Robin Hood's Stride**
3 miles (4.8km)   64

walk 14: **High Tor & the Heights of Abraham**
4½ miles (7.2km)   68

walk 15: **Cromford & the High Peak Incline**
3½ miles (5.6km)   72

walk 16: **Tissington & Parwich**
3¾ miles (6km)   76

walk 17: **Ilam Hall**
4½ miles (7.2km)   80

walk 18: **Three Shires Head**
4 miles (6.4km)   84

walk 19: **Viator's Bridge, Milldale**
2¼ miles (3.6km)   88

walk 20: **Thor's Cave**
4 miles (6.4km)   92

Introduction

Walking in the Peak District

Walking in the Peak District

When walking in the Peak District you can encounter some quite different types of terrain. Probably the easiest walking of all is on the limestone plateau where stone stiles and green lanes indicate the way. In the dales, paths wander through shady woodland and follow bubbling trout rivers. In the north, the unpredictable weather makes navigation across the trackless moors quite difficult. Gritstone edges above the Derwent, or the lower heather moors, are more straightforward and the footpaths are easier to follow.

Walking is a pastime which can fulfil the needs of everyone. You can adapt it to suit your own preferences and it is one of the healthiest of activities. This guide is for those who just want to walk a few miles. It really doesn't take long to find yourself in some lovely countryside. All the walks are five miles or less so should easily be completed in under three hours. Walking can be anything from an individual pastime to a family stroll, or maybe a group of friends enjoying the fresh air and open spaces of our countryside. There is no need for walking to be competitive and, to get the most from a walk, it shouldn't be regarded simply as a means of covering a given distance in the shortest possible time.

What is the Peak District?

The title 'Peak District' is something of a misnomer. The name 'Peak', in fact, refers to a tribe who lived in the area in ancient times. In the year 924, a cleric writing about the hills and dales of what is now North Derbyshire, referred to the inhabitants as living in 'Peaclond' and the name seems to have stuck.

There are really two Peak Districts – Dark and White. The two areas are so completely different that, when standing on the breezy limestone plateau of the White Peak, it is hard to imagine that the untamed wilderness of Bleaklow and Kinder Scout are not far away. Broadly speaking, the Peak District can be sub-divided into six distinct areas;

- The most northerly is the wildest and covers the moors above Saddleworth and the Longdendale Valley with the huge spread of Bleaklow filling the space between Longdendale and the Snake Pass.

- Kinder Scout is a vast boggy plateau bordered to its south by Edale and the graceful sweep of the Mam Tor - Rushup Edge Ridge.

- To the east, rising above the Derwent Valley, there is a long escarpment which is clearly defined by a series of gritstone edges backed by heather moorland.

- In the west, gritstone crags range from The Roaches above Leek to Windgather Rocks and Castle Naze on the northern limits. High open moors offer miles of lesser known walking. Tranquil wooded valleys cutting the western moors are excellent places to walk on hot summer days.

- Limestone makes its most northerly appearance in dramatic cliffs and knolls above Castleton, a place of caves and ancient lead mines. South of Castleton are some of the highest villages in the White Peak. They can expect to be cut off by deep snow for several days during most winters.

- The limestone plateau to the southwest of the A6 is incised by deep valleys and is judged by many to be the prettiest part of the Peak. It is certainly a zone of contrasts where the lush pastures of the rolling uplands have been grazed by cattle since time immemorial. Rivers run pure and clear and they are full of lively trout.

People came early to the Peak. Settling first on the treeless limestone plateau, they left mysterious mounds and stone circles. The circle at Arbor Low between Hartington and Youlgreave was probably the most important. Certainly its surrounding earthworks indicate its significance. Arbor Low is unique as the stones lie flat, unlike the more familiar uprights associated with other circles.

Peak District landscape

During the Middle Ages, most of the lands were owned by various monasteries. They continued to exploit the lead resources, which was then very much in demand both as a roofing material and for constructing pipes to supply water into a growing number of monastic establishments. The monks opened large tracts of arable grazing and produced wool to clothe an expanding population. Farms which today have the word Grange as part of their name, were owned by rich monasteries until their dissolution by Henry VIII.

Great houses have been built in the Peak. Some are well known, like Chatsworth with its parkland, which was landscaped by Capability Brown, or Haddon Hall – a uniquely preserved medieval country house. There are also many lesser-known stately homes throughout the district which are just as interesting. Most are in private hands, like Tissington Hall which has been owned by the same family for generations. Hartington Hall, a fine example of a Jacobean yeoman's house is now a youth hostel as is Ham Hall which is an early Victorian mansion preserved by the National Trust.

Visitors to the Peak can buy jewellery made from Blue John, a semi precious stone found only beneath Treak Cliff, near Castleton. Another Peak novelty is the Bakewell Pudding (never call it a tart!). This delicacy was first made accidentally by a 19th century cook working in the Rutland Arms Hotel. Very fine.

Famous writers have penned the virtues of the Peak but none has better links than Izaak Walton (author of 'The Compleat Angler' published in 1653), who fished The Dove with the poet Charles Cotton.

Industry has always made its mark. Pack horse, or 'jaggers' tracks can still be followed on foot over the northern moors. Saltways crossed the southern dales. Water-powered mills in the early part of the Industrial Revolution brought textile production to the dales. Fluorspar, a nuisance to the early lead miners, is now extracted by open cast mining and used as a flux in steel making and as the basis for a number of chemicals.

Today, without any doubt, it is quarrying which makes the greatest industrial impact on the face of the Peak District. Limestone, suitable either as road aggregates or for cement making, is often only found in scenically attractive areas and, as a result, the quarries can make an ugly scar on the landscape unless they are carefully monitored.

Geology

The rocks which made the foundations of the Peak District were laid down millions of years ago in a warm sea. Miriads of sea creatures living on the slimy bottom built up the great depth of limestone. Tropical lagoons were fringed by coral reefs which, through time, have become the rounded hills of Thorpe Cloud, Parkhouse and Chrome Hills in Dovedale. Minor volcanic activity took place during this time. The best examples of this can be found in the small outcrops of basalt near Castleton and in the dolerite quarry which is part of the Tideswell Dale Nature Trail. Lead found its way in gaseous form, through minute cracks in the underlying rocks, laying down the basis of what became a major industry thousands of centuries later. Copper was also deposited in this way, occurring beneath Ecton Hill in the Manifold valley.

A mighty river delta flooded into the tropical sea, depositing mud and sand which consolidated to make the gritstones of the Dark Peak and the shales of Mam Tor.

Gradually, the layers of limestone and gritstone bulged from pressures deep within the earth and the middle and edges split. Ice action later honed the land into the beginning of the Peak District's rocky pattern. At the end of the Ice Age, huge volumes of melt water continued this shaping. The water carved caverns within the limestone of Castleton and Matlock as well as the pot holes of Eldon and it also created the beautiful dales. The land tilted as it buckled to give west facing gritstone outcrops on both sides of the Peak.

Wildlife in the Peak District

Grouse spend their hardy lives on the high moors of the Dark Peak feeding on the tender shoots of young heather. Their tough existence is rudely shattered for four months of every year beginning on the 'Glorious Twelfth of August'. Not so common, and regrettably often shot by mistake, are their cousins the black grouse. Birds of prey have their chosen areas and many migrants, some quite rare, visit quieter sanctuaries on the moors from time to time. Mountain hares are common despite an inability to quickly shed their winter camouflage once the snows have gone. Foxes live a frugal life, mainly dependent upon voles and other small creatures. Plant life on the acid moors has to be tough to combat the extreme weather conditions. Heathers, coarse grass and berry plants such as bilberry, cloudberry and crowberry manage to survive in this harsh environment.

The limestone plateau is much more gentle. It is mainly given over to grazing and masses of colourful flowers still fill the hayfields and road verges. Scabious, meadow cranesbill and other plants, which were once scarce, have made a recent comeback in fields where far-sighted farmers have moved back to natural and cheaper methods of fertilising the land. Plant, and to a certain extent animal life, in the dales depend on the underlying strata. The Upper Derwent and its tributaries flow mostly through shale and gritstone. Forests planted around the Derwent Reservoirs are a major feature and offer homes to woodland birds and a few deer as well as the smaller carnivorous animals. In the limestone dales, trees were once cut down for fuel but they are plentiful today and, in some instances, they are crowding other plant life. In Dovedale, a courageous scheme has removed much of the invasive woodland to recreate more open vistas. Plant life on the craggy scree-covered hillsides is mostly dwarf and with an almost alpine quality. But the dales are best known for their trout streams. Not only do game fish breed in their clear waters, but crayfish, a crustacean which needs pure water, is found beneath the rocks of most of the rivers in the dales.

The Peak District National Park

The Peak District National Park was designated in 1951 and extends over 542 square miles (1404 sq.km). Divided into two uniquely different zones, with wild gritstone moors to the north and gentler limestone uplands and dales to the south, it is surrounded by millions of people living in the industrial areas of England. Due to the advent of motorways the Peak is accessible to the bulk of the population in under two hours. The Peak District was the first National Park and is the most visited.

Administration of the park is controlled by a committee composed, on a proportional basis of representatives of the surrounding County, City, District and Borough Councils as well as members appointed by the Secretary of State for the Environment.

One of the statutory functions of a Park Authority is the appointment of full-time and voluntary Park Rangers. These are people with particular knowledge of some aspects of the local environment who are available

to give help and advice to visitors. Other functions of the Ranger Service include giving assistance to local farmers in such matters as rebuilding damaged walls to prevent stock from straying and leading guided walks from one of the Information Centres. Permanent Information Centres open all year are based at Edale, Castleton, Bakewell and Fairholmes. There are other information centres throughout the National Park.

One of the first tasks the Peak District National Park set itself after its formation in 1951 was to negotiate access agreements. These were not always straightforward but, by careful and diplomatic negotiation, agreements have been reached with farmers and landowners giving free access to most of the high moors of the Dark Peak. Large parts of moorland, including Kinder Scout, are open to unrestricted walking and rock climbing apart from a few days in summer when sections of the moors are closed for grouse shooting. Notices are published locally showing the dates when the moors are closed and there are also signposts giving dates at access points to the moors.

Losehill Hall National Park Learning and Environmental Conference Centre is a converted Victorian mansion which is set in spaciously wooded grounds to the south of Lose Hill. Residential and day courses are held on a wide variety of topics ranging from environmental studies, archaeology and the National Park and the pressures it faces, to hill walking, cycling, caving and more specialised subjects.

Walking tips & guidance

Safety
As with all other outdoor activities, walking is safe provided a few simple commonsense rules are followed:

• Make sure you are fit enough to complete the walk;

• Always try to let others know where you intend going, especially if you are walking alone;

• Be clothed adequately for the weather and always wear suitable footwear;

• Always allow plenty of time for the walk, especially if it is longer or harder than you have done before;

• Whatever the distance you plan to walk, always allow plenty of daylight hours unless you are absolutely certain of the route;

• If mist or bad weather come on unexpectedly, do not panic but instead try to remember the last certain feature which you have passed (road, farm, wood, etc.). Then work out your route from that point on the map but be sure of your route before continuing;

- Do not dislodge stones on the high edges: there may be climbers or other walkers on the lower crags and slopes;

- Unfortunately, accidents can happen even on the easiest of walks. If this should be the case and you need the help of others, make sure that the injured person is safe in a place where no further injury is likely to occur. For example, the injured person should not be left on a steep hillside or in danger from falling rocks. If you have a mobile phone and there is a signal, call for assistance. If, however, you are unable to contact help by mobile and you cannot leave anyone with the injured person, and even if they are conscious, try to leave a written note explaining their injuries and whatever you have done in the way of first aid treatment. Make sure you know exactly where you left them and then go to find assistance. Make your way to a telephone, dial 999 and ask for the police or mountain rescue. Unless the accident has happened within easy access of a road, it is the responsibility of the police to arrange evacuation. Always give accurate directions on how to find the casualty and, if possible, give an indication of the injuries involved;

- When walking in open country, learn to keep an eye on the immediate foreground while you admire the scenery or plan the route ahead. This may sound difficult but will enhance your walking experience;

- It's best to walk at a steady pace, always on the flat of the feet as this is less tiring. Try not to walk directly up or downhill. A zigzag route is a more comfortable way of negotiating a slope. Running directly downhill is a major cause of erosion on popular hillsides;

- When walking along a country road, walk on the right, facing the traffic. The exception to this rule is, when approaching a blind bend, the walker should cross over to the left and so have a clear view and also be seen in both directions;

- Finally, always park your car where it will not cause inconvenience to other road users or prevent a farmer from gaining access to his fields. Take any valuables with you or lock them out of sight in the car.

Equipment

Equipment, including clothing, footwear and rucksacks, is essentially a personal thing and depends on several factors, such as the type of activity planned, the time of year, and weather likely to be encountered.

All too often, a novice walker will spend money on a fashionable jacket but will skimp when it comes to buying footwear or a comfortable rucksack. Blistered and tired feet quickly remove all enjoyment from even the most exciting walk and a poorly balanced rucksack will soon feel as though you are carrying a ton of bricks. Well designed equipment is not only more comfortable but, being better made, it is longer lasting.

Clothing should be adequate for the day. In summer, remember to protect your head and neck, which are particularly vulnerable in a strong sun and use sun screen. Wear light woollen socks and lightweight boots or strong shoes. A spare pullover and waterproofs carried in the rucksack should, however, always be there in case you need them.

Winter wear is a much more serious affair. Remember that once the body starts to lose heat, it becomes much less efficient. Jeans are particularly unsuitable for winter wear and can sometimes even be downright dangerous.

Waterproof clothing is an area where it pays to buy the best you can afford. Make sure that the jacket is loose-fitting, windproof and has a generous hood. Waterproof overtrousers will not only offer complete protection in the rain but they are also windproof. Do not be misled by flimsy nylon 'showerproof' items. Remember, too, that garments made from rubberised or plastic material are heavy to carry and wear and they trap body condensation. Your rucksack should have wide, padded carrying straps for comfort.

It is important to wear boots that fit well or shoes with a good moulded sole – blisters can ruin any walk! Woollen socks are much more comfortable than any other fibre. Your clothes should be comfortable and not likely to catch on twigs and bushes.

It is important to carry a compass, preferably one of the 'Silva' type as well as this guide. A smaller scale map covering a wider area can add to the enjoyment of a walk. Binoculars are not essential but are very useful for spotting distant stiles and give added interest to viewpoints and wildlife. Although none of the walks in this guide venture too far from civilisation, on a hot day even the shortest of walks can lead to dehydration so a bottle of water is advisable.

Finally, a small first aid kit is an invaluable help in coping with cuts and other small injuries.

Public Rights of Way

In 1949, the National Parks and Access to the Countryside Act tidied up the law covering rights of way. Following public consultation, maps were drawn up by the Countryside Authorities of England and Wales to show all the rights of way. Copies of these maps are available for public inspection and are invaluable when trying to resolve doubts over little-used footpaths. Once on the map, the right of way is irrefutable.

Right of way means that anyone may walk freely on a defined footpath or ride a horse or pedal cycle along a public bridleway. No one may interfere with this right and the walker is within his rights if he removes any obstruction along the route, provided that he has not set out purposely with the intention of removing that obstruction. All obstructions should be reported to the local Highways Authority.

In England and Wales rights of way fall into three main categories:

- Public Footpaths – for walkers only;

- Bridleways – for passage on foot, horseback, or bicycle;

- Byways – for all the above and for motorized vehicles

Free access to footpaths and bridleways does mean that certain guidelines should be followed as a courtesy to those who live and work in the area. For example, you should only sit down to picnic where it does not interfere with other walkers or the landowner. All gates must be kept closed to prevent stock from straying and dogs must be kept under close control – usually this is interpreted as meaning that they should be kept on a leash. Motor vehicles must not be driven along a public footpath or bridleway without the landowner's consent.

A farmer can put a docile mature beef bull with a herd of cows or heifers, in a field crossed by a public footpath. Beef bulls such as Herefords (usually brown/red colour) are unlikely to be upset by passers by but dairy bulls, like the black and white Friesian, can be dangerous by nature. It is, therefore, illegal for a farmer to let a dairy bull roam loose in a field open to public access.

The Countryside and Rights of Way Act 2000 (the 'right to roam') allows access on foot to areas of legally defined 'open country' – mountain, moor, downland, heath and registered common land. You will find these areas shaded orange on the maps in this guide. It does not allow freedom to walk anywhere. It also increases protection for Sites of Special Scientific Interest, improves wildlife enforcement legislation and allows better management of Areas of Outstanding Natural Beauty.

Pennine Way

The Country Code

The Country Code has been designed not as a set of hard and fast rules, although they do have the backing of the law, but as a statement of commonsense. The code is a gentle reminder of how to behave in the countryside. Walkers should walk with the intention of leaving the place exactly as it was before they arrived. There is a saying that a good walker 'leaves only footprints and takes only photographs', which really sums up the code perfectly.

Never walk more than two abreast on a footpath as you will erode more ground by causing an unnatural widening of paths. Also try to avoid the spread of trodden ground around a boggy area. Mud soon cleans off boots but plant life is slow to grow back once it has been worn away.

Have respect for everything in the countryside, be it those beautiful flowers found along the way or a farmer's gate which is difficult to close.

Stone walls were built at a time when labour costs were a fraction of those today and the special skills required to build or repair them have almost disappeared. Never climb over or onto stone walls; always use stiles and gates.

Dogs which chase sheep can cause them to lose their lambs and a farmer is within his rights if he shoots a dog which he believes is worrying his stock.

The moors and woodlands are often tinder dry in summer, so take care not to start a fire. A fire caused by something as simple as a discarded cigarette can burn for weeks, once it gets deep down into the underlying peat.

When walking across fields or enclosed land, make sure that you read the map carefully and avoid trespassing. As a rule, the line of a footpath or right of way, even when it is not clearly defined on the ground, can usually be followed by lining up stiles or gates.

Obviously flowers and plants encountered on a walk should not be taken but left for others passing to enjoy. To use the excuse 'I have only taken a few' is futile. If everyone only took a few the countryside would be devastated. If young wild animals are encountered they should be left well alone. For instance, if a fawn or a deer calf is discovered lying still in the grass it would be wrong to assume that it has been abandoned. Mothers hide their offspring while they go away to graze and browse and return to them at feeding time. If the animals are touched it could mean that they will be abandoned as the human scent might deter the mother from returning to her offspring. Similarly with baby birds, who have not yet mastered flight; they may appear to have been abandoned but often are being watched by their parents who might be waiting for a walker to pass on before coming out to give flight lesson two!

What appear to be harmful snakes should not be killed because firstly the 'snake' could be a slow worm, which looks like a snake but is really a harmless legless lizard, and second, even if it were an adder (they are quite common) it will escape if given the opportunity. Adders are part of the pattern of nature and should not be persecuted. They rarely bite unless they are handled; a foolish act, which is not uncommon; or trodden on, which is rare, as the snakes are usually basking in full view and are very quick to escape.

Map reading

Some people find map reading so easy that they can open a map and immediately relate it to the area of countryside in which they are standing. To others, a map is as unintelligible as ancient Greek! A map is an accurate but flat picture of the three-dimensional features of the countryside. Features such as roads, streams, woodland and buildings are relatively easy to identify, either from their shape or position. Heights, on the other hand, can be difficult to interpret from the single dimension of a map. The Ordnance Survey 1:25,000 mapping used in this guide shows the contours at 5 metre intervals. Summits and spot heights are also shown.

The best way to estimate the angle of a slope, as shown on any map, is to remember that if the contour lines come close together then the slope is steep – the closer together the contours the steeper the slope.

Learn the symbols for features shown on the map and, when starting out on a walk, line up the map with one or more features, which are recognisable both from the map and on the ground. In this way, the map will be correctly positioned relative to the terrain. It should then only be necessary to look from the map towards the footpath or objective of your walk and then make for it! This process is also useful for determining your position at any time during the walk.

Let's take the skill of map reading one stage further: sometimes there are no easily recognisable features nearby: there may be the odd clump of trees and a building or two but none of them can be related exactly to the map. This is a frequent occurrence but there is a simple answer to the problem and this is where the use of a compass comes in. Simply place the map on the ground, or other flat surface, with the compass held gently above the map. Turn the map until the edge is parallel to the line of the compass needle, which should point to the top of the map. Lay the compass on the map and adjust the position of both, making sure that the compass needle still points to the top of the map and is parallel to the edge. By this method, the map is orientated in a north-south alignment. To find your position on the map, look out for prominent features and draw imaginary lines from them down on to the map. Your position is where these lines cross. This method of map reading takes a little practice before you can become proficient but it is worth the effort.

How to use this book

This book contains route maps and descriptions for 20 walks, with areas of interest indicated by symbols (see below). For each walk particular points of interest are denoted by a number both in the text and on the map (where the number appears in a circle). In the text the route instructions are prefixed by a capital letter. We recommend that you read the whole description, including the fact box at the start of each walk, before setting out.

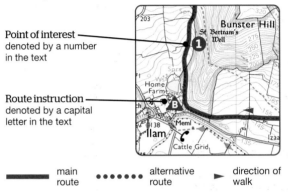

Point of interest — denoted by a number in the text

Route instruction — denoted by a capital letter in the text

━━━━━ main route

●●●●●●● alternative route

► direction of walk

Key to walk symbols

At the start of each walk there is a series of symbols that indicate particular areas of interest associated with the route.

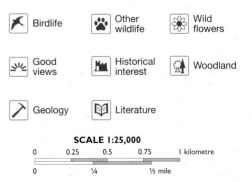

Birdlife	Other wildlife	Wild flowers
Good views	Historical interest	Woodland
Geology	Literature	

SCALE 1:25,000

0   0.25   0.5   0.75   1 kilometre

0   ¼   ½ mile

Please note the scale for walk maps is 1:25,000 unless otherwise stated
North is always at the top of the page

> **"** The route of this lovely walk takes in the Ladybower Wood, a beautiful upland oakwood, at the edge of which you may be able to spot red grouse or even the mountain hare **"**

Here is a chance to experience the Derwent moors and edges at close hand. Both the wide footpath from Cutthroat Bridge and the second, which it joins near Moscar House, are easy to follow and use routes which predate the busy A57 road by many centuries. An airy track crosses the rocky escarpment of Derwent Edge where there are enticing views of the wild moors beyond Ladybower. Dropping down through a mature pine forest, the final leg of the route conveniently passes the welcome sight of the Ladybower Inn.

Derwent Moors

Derwent Moors

Route instructions

A ▶ Park in the large layby and walk down the road, then turn right on the rocky path. Turn sharp right beneath power lines. Cross the stream and follow a grassy path across the moor.

B ▶ At the gateway overlooking the stream and farm, turn sharp left and follow the stone wall. Beyond the upper wall, the path crosses the moor, following a line of shooting butts.

C ▶ Turn left along the crest of the rocky moorland escarpment.

1 Viewpoint. 'Wheel Stones' or the 'Coach & Horses', are the first of a line of distinctive gritstone outcrops along Derwent Edge. It is possible to extend the walk to make a closer inspection of the outcrops.

D ▶ Turn right and go down the hillside. Follow the tracks to the left of the boundary wall, through mature pine forest.

2 Viewpoint looking across the northern arm of Ladybower Reservoir. The building of the reservoir between 1935 and 1943 resulted in the drowning of the villages of Ashopton and Derwent and created what was, at the time, the largest reservoir in Britain. During exceptionally dry summers the foundations of

Plan your walk

DISTANCE: 4¾ miles (7.6km)

TIME: 2½ hours

START/END: SK214874 Car park at Cutthroat Bridge

TERRAIN: Easy / Moderate;

MAPS:
OS Explorer OL 1;
OS Landranger 110

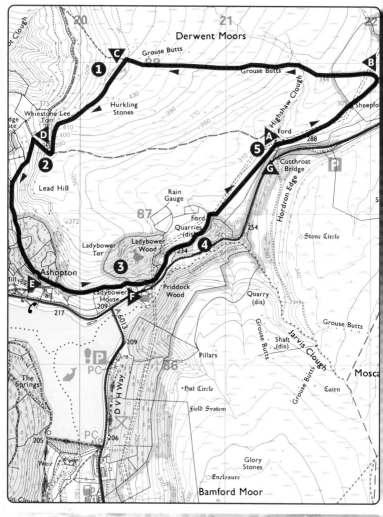

Ladybower Reservoir

Derwent Moors

Derwent village can still be seen. The last time this happened was in 2004 when some remains of the church gateposts and a bridge over the River Derwent were still clearly visible. Ashopton was located to the south of the A57 viaduct and was more extensively demolished in 1943 before the reservoir was flooded. What little remained was covered in silt many years ago.

E Leave the forest and bear left, above a group of farm buildings, and go through two gates.

F Turn right for the Ladybower Inn, otherwise bear left at the footpath junction (return to this point if visiting the pub). Climb the rocky path to the open moor.

3 Ladybower Woods is a nature reserve owned and cared for by the Derbyshire Wildlife Trust. It is one of the few upland oakwoods left in the Peak District.

4 Viewpoint. Look back at the surprise view of the lower section of Ladybower Reservoir.

G Turn right at the footpath junction to rejoin the A57.

5 Cutthroat Bridge. The name commemorates the spot where a man was found barely alive with a wound to his throat in 1635. He died in Bamford Hall two days later. The bridge wasn't built until 1821 but the gruesome event is remembered in its name.

Ashopton Viaduct, Ladybower Reservoir

> **"** The route climbs from the small village of Combs and offers views of Kinder Scout in the distance **"**

The walk starts and finishes at the Beehive Inn, a focal point of the pleasant village of Combs, which nestles snugly beneath the wild moorland of Combs Moss, a little known outlier of the Dark Peak.

Combs

Combs Reservoir

Route instructions

A Follow the Dove Holes road away from the front of the Beehive Inn.

B Where the road bears left, turn right along a lane through Rye Flatt farmyard.

1 Viewpoint. The private grouse moor of Combs Moss is in front. To the left are the crags of Castle Naze, a favourite training ground for local rock climbers. Behind the rocks and out of sight, a solid earthen bank marks the limits of an Iron Age fort.

C A few yards beyond a modern bungalow where the lane bears left to Allstone Lee Farm, continue ahead through a gate and

along a field path signposted to White Hall.

D Cross two adjacent footbridges, one stone and the other wood. Climb a series of fields using stiles and gateways.

2 Viewpoint. The slopes below the building on the skyline to the left are covered by bracken which will not grow on the windy heights beyond the moorland edge. That region is given over to heather and bilberry.

E Turn sharp right through Combshead farmyard. Go through a gateway and turn left uphill, beside a wire fence above a shallow gully. Keep to the pathless route

Plan your walk

DISTANCE: 4 miles (6.4km)

TIME: 2 hours

START/END: SK042786

TERRAIN: Moderate; muddy sections

MAPS:
OS Explorer OL 24;
OS Landranger 119

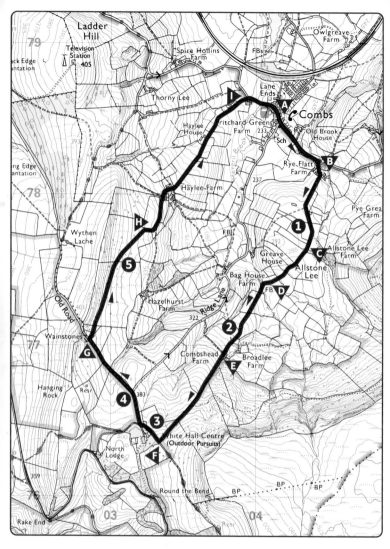

by using stiles in field boundaries.

▶F Go through a gate and turn right on to a moorland road, then right again beyond the hall. After 250yds (230m) keep left at a road junction.

3 White Hall is an Outdoor Pursuits Centre run by Derbyshire County Council and was the first Outdoor

Combs

Education Centre to be established in the country.

4 The road follows the route between Roman Arnemetia (Buxton) and Mancunium (Manchester).

G Turn right opposite the modernised farmhouse of Wainstones. Go past a ruined barn and out along the rough field track beneath a stony ridge.

5 Viewpoint. Combs village fits snugly in a wide hollow beneath Combs Moss. In the distance, to your half left, is Kinder Scout and its outliers.

H After crossing three rough fields, bear right downhill to a walled lane. Follow it left to Haylee Farm. Go right, through the farmyard and left along a leafy lane.

I Turn right at the lane end and follow the road back to the village.

Kinder Scout

> **Gentle walk taking in some attractive upland limestone scenery**

Lands of the northern Peak were once a royal hunting preserve, or forest, controlled by harsh laws. Cruel punishments were inflicted on anyone other than the nobility who was caught taking the King's game. Today the only link with the past is the name of the village, Peak Forest – a scattering of farms and sturdy cottages, fortunately neglected by motorists hurrying along the A623. Peak Forest once had a certain notoriety when it became a kind of English Gretna Green, permitting eloping couples to marry in its parish church.

Peak Forest

View of Rushup Edge

Route instructions

A Park along the Old Dam road. Cross the A623 opposite the Devonshire Arms pub and turn right through a small wooden gate near an old iron hand pump. Follow the faint path over a series of fields, using stiles to keep to the route.

B Go through stiles and a wicket gate to the left of Dam Dale Farm. Keep to the left of an old wall along the dale bottom.

1 Viewpoint. Dam Dale – a typical upland limestone dale where the plant life is more closely related to an alpine environment.

C Turn left, uphill, along a walled grassy lane.

D Turn left immediately before the road junction. Go through a gate, following the direction of a signpost. There is only a faint path at times but the line can be followed by careful use of stiles and occasional waymarks.

2 Viewpoint. Peak Forest lies in the hollow below Eldon Hill. Rushup Edge is in the background, marking the division between the southerly limestones and gritstone of the Dark Peak.

E Turn right on to the road and follow it beyond its second, uphill hairpin. Take care as there will be vehicles passing.

Plan your walk

DISTANCE: 4¼ miles (6.8km)

TIME: 2¼ hours

START/END: SK114793 Peak Forest

TERRAIN: Easy

MAPS:
OS Explorer OL 24;
OS Landranger 110

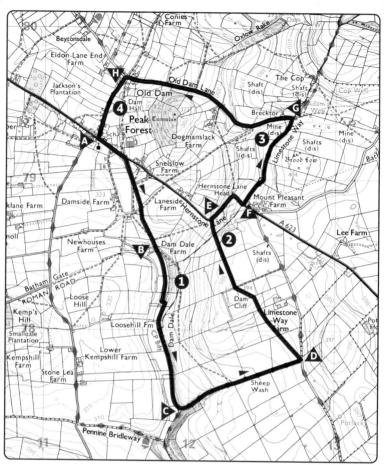

F Go left through a metal gate at the side of a belt of trees, sheltering Mount Pleasant Farm. Walk along the enclosed grassy lane.

3 Humps and hollows in the open space at the lane end denote one-time lead mining in the area.

G Turn left along the quiet lane and walk down into Old Dam.

H Turn left at the T junction and return to the starting point.

4 The duck pond on the left was a man-made communal watering place for village cattle in the days before piped water reached the surrounding farms.

Peak Forest

A notable feature of Peak Forest is Eldon Hole; a 197ft (60m) deep chasm in the side of Eldon Hill to the north of the village. Access from the village is via Eldon Lane, and is about a half-hour walk. It is a favourite of potholers.

Pennine Bridleway

> Tranquil walk which offers some lovely views of Overdale Nature Reserve where meadow pipit, skylark, whinchat, wheatear and curlew may be seen

Quiet lanes climb the windswept heights to moors which offer unrivalled views across the southern boundary of the Dark Peak. This easy walk covers a part of the Peak which is often neglected by walkers. An added attraction is the opportunity to watch gliders from nearby Hucklow Edge seeking updrafts along the heights. Gliders are the only manmade intrusion in this area of solitude.

Edale valley

Shatton Moor

Hope Valley

Route instructions

A Parking is sparse in Shatton village so take care not to impede other road users. Follow the sunken Townfield Lane to the open fields.

B Turn right through a gate at the lane end and follow a field track to the right of the boundary hedge.

C Turn left through a gate. Follow the line of electricity poles as far as Elmore Farm. Yellow waymarks to the right of the farmyard indicate the route. Beyond the farm, keep to the right of the field boundary.

1 The view of the Edale Valley and Mam Tor Ridge is only marred by the intrusive chimney of the cement works.

D Cross a stone stile and turn left, uphill along a rough bridleway. Follow this walled track along the broad grassy ridge to a col above Over Dale.

2 Grey Ditch and Rebellion Knoll. The prominent earthwork on the right of the track reaches down to Bradwell. This is an ancient boundary but its links with Rebellion Knoll, the small rise beyond Grey Ditch, are unclear. It could refer to a rebellion of slaves in the Roman lead mines. There was an administrative fort at Navio, near Brough.

Plan your walk

DISTANCE: 4½ miles (7.2km)

TIME: 2¼ hours

START/END: SK201825 Shatton

TERRAIN: Easy; one 775ft (236m) climb

MAPS: OS Explorer OL 1; OS Landranger 110

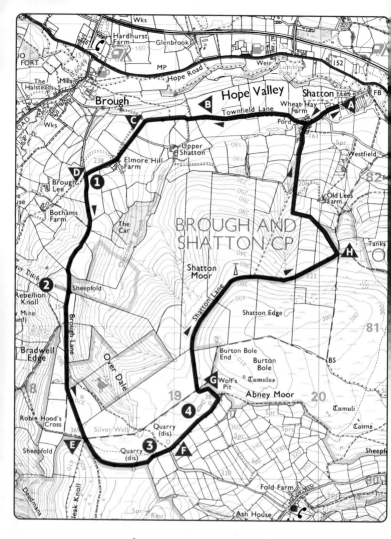

E Keep left along the sandy track and head towards the open moor.

F Walk on, continuing ahead at the junction of bridleways.

3 Viewpoint. Bretton Clough ('home of the Britons') is to the south.

4 Viewpoint. Overdale Nature Reserve fills the valley head and is the haunt of moorland birds.

Shatton Moor

G Follow the direction of the bridleway signpost to Shatton. Turn right at Wolf's Pit and join a walled lane. Follow this round the shoulder of Shatton Edge, past the conspicuous TV booster mast.

H Bear left downhill on the metalled road back to Shatton.

Hope Valley

66 Easy walk with some boggy sections, with a relatively gentle climb up to Higger Tor where there are lovely views over the Derwent Valley and heather clad moors 99

There are many enigmas in the Peak District: stone circles, cairns and burial mounds were left by a community which had no means of conveying their purpose to us. Possibly of slightly later antiquity, Carl Wark hill fort hints of the need for tribes of the time to protect themselves from attack. We cannot tell whether this fort is Iron Age or even post Roman, but what is certain is that it was built in such a way that even the siege of time has had little effect.

Carl Wark & Higger Tor

Longshaw Estate

Route instructions

A From the Longshaw Estate car park, walk through the narrow belt of beechwoods to the estate lodge. Cross the B6521 to enter a stretch of mixed woodland flanking the A625 below the Fox House Inn.

B Join the A625 at Burbage Bridge. Follow the road as far as the Toad's Mouth rock.

1 Toad's Mouth. This rock stands at the side of the road. When viewed from below, the projecting snout and carved eye are said to resemble the head of a toad but you will not be alone if you feel that the likeness is closer to a moray eel!

C Look out for a stile set back from the road about 100yds (90m) past Toad's Mouth rock. Cross it and follow an upward path across the moor, through heather and bracken. Aim for the prominent knoll of Carl Wark.

2 Carl Wark hill fort. The massive stone walls of the outer perimeter of this defensive point have stood the test of time. Traces of hut foundations and water troughs can still be seen. Notice also how the walls overshadow the two entrance points.

D Cross the low col beyond the fort and climb the wide peaty path towards the rocks of Higger Tor.

Plan your walk

DISTANCE: 3¾ miles (6km)

TIME: 2 hours

START/END: SK267801 Longshaw Estate car park

TERRAIN: Easy / Moderate; boggy sections

MAPS: OS Explorer OL 24; OS Landranger 119

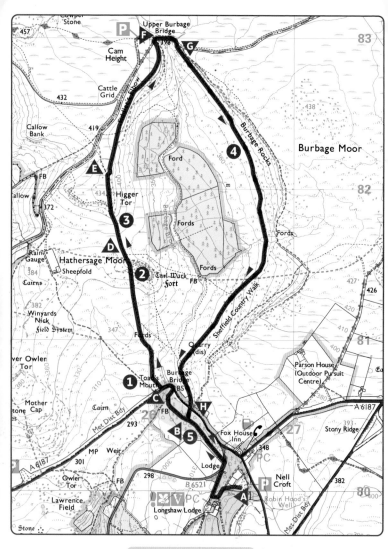

3 Viewpoint. Carl Wark is below on its natural eminence with the Derwent Valley and heather clad moors stretching into the distance.

E Clamber across the summit rocks and follow the escarpment to the right. Follow the moorland path parallel to Fiddler's Elbow road.

Carl Wark & Higger Tor

F Cross both of the streams beneath the bridges and join the green track.

G Follow the track past a series of abandoned gritstone quarries as far as the main road.

4 Viewpoint. Burbage Brook follows its rocky way from its moorland birth. A plantation of mixed conifers adds to the pleasant scene.

H Cross the road and go through a kissing gate. Pick up the path and follow back through the trees to the car park.

Moors above Higger Tor

> The route follows a fairly steep path alongside the rocky Burbage Brook, which cuts through beautiful ancient oak woodland, opening out to reveal distant views of Kinder Scout, Win Hill and Bleaklow

A deep rocky gorge, surrounded by ancient oak woodland, and a splendid Victorian hunting lodge screened by rhododendrons are the main features on this walk. The views are far ranging and yet contrast with the arboreal beauty of Padley Gorge. If time and energies permit, this walk can be regarded as an extension to walk 5, Carl Wark.

Padley Gorge

Longshaw Estate

Plan your walk

DISTANCE: 3¾ miles (6km)

TIME: 2 hours

START/END: SK267801 Longshaw Estate car park

TERRAIN: Moderate; 600ft (183m) descent and ascent

MAPS:
OS Explorer OL 24;
OS Landranger 119

Route instructions

A From the Longshaw Estate car park, follow the woodland path to the estate lodge at the side of the B6521 Frogatt road.

B Cross the road and follow the path down to Burbage Brook.

C Cross the stream by a log bridge and turn left, downstream.

D Go ahead at the path junction, walking down a steep hill through ancient oak woods lining Padley Gorge. Try to keep the stream in sight below and on the left, ignoring side turnings along this rocky woodland path.

1 View of Padley Gorge.

This wild forested ravine is a reminder of what our native countryside once looked like.

E Go through a kissing gate and down a rough lane past groups of houses. Turn left at the bottom and follow the lane over the railway bridge to a café.

2 The mill, which is now a private house, relied upon Burbage Brook to power its wheels.

F Turn left immediately beyond the café, through a kissing gate and climb up to the road.

G Turn left on to the road and, after a few yards, turn right over a low stone stile.

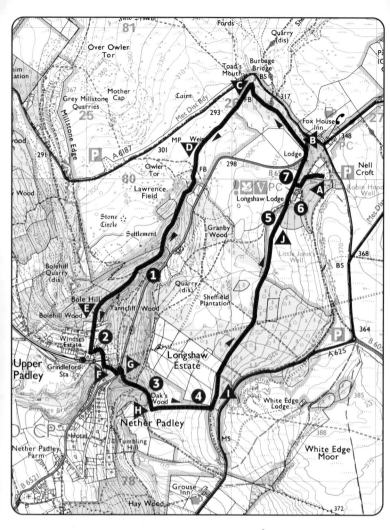

Climb the steep woodland path, following the rocky course of the stream.

3 Viewpoint. Look back across the intervening woodland towards the Derwent Valley with Eyam Moor in the distance.

H After emerging from the woods, turn left uphill beside a stream tributary, eventually joining a worn flagged path.

4 Viewpoint. The Upper Derwent stretches into the distance. Kinder Scout, Win

Padley Gorge

Hill and Bleaklow form the final backcloth.

▶ Climb a stone stile and turn left along the woodland drive. Follow this level track in and out of planted woodland and open grassland dotted by clumps of semi-wild rhododendrons.

▶ Go through a narrow gate to the left of Longshaw Lodge, follow the path around the foot of the 'ha-ha' back to the car park.

5 Viewpoint. In May or June, pink and crimson flowers of the rhododendron bushes make an attractive foreground to the view.

6 Longshaw Lodge. This Victorian hunting lodge and the surrounding estate is now owned by the National Trust.

7 The low wall is a 'ha-ha'. Normally a 'ha-ha' is topped by a formal lawn which prevents animals from entering the garden, leaving the view from the house unspoiled.

Longshaw Estate

66 This four mile walk takes you past Nelson's Monument nearby to which there are three boulders known as the Victory, Defiance and Sovereign, all of which took part in the Battle of Trafalgar 99

Two monoliths erected in memory of Nelson and Wellington make excellent route markers for this walk. The route crosses stark gritstone edges on the skyline above Bar Brook, which offer magnificent views of the surrounding moors and parkland.

Birchen Edge

Birchen Edge

Route instructions

A Park near the Robin Hood Inn above the A619 Chesterfield road. Walk past the adjoining cottage and go through the gate on the left. Follow the rocky, woodland path uphill, aiming for the crest of Birchen Edge.

B Take care on reaching the lower part of the crag and follow the path through a rocky gap. Turn left along the summit rocks.

1 Nelson's Monument. Nearby are three boulders, each shaped like the bow of a man-of-war. They are fancifully named Victory, Defiance and Sovereign – all ships at the Battle of Trafalgar.

2 Viewpoint. Chatsworth House and its park fills the valley. To the left is the largest expanse of grouse moor in the Southern Pennines.

C At the triangulation pillar, turn left downhill through the narrow gap in the crag. Turn right along a narrow moorland path following occasional wooden marker posts.

D Climb a ladder stile and turn left on to the road. Follow it with great care across the busy A621 Sheffield road. Walk uphill, opposite, for about 150yds (137m).

E Go left through a gate

Plan your walk

DISTANCE: 4 miles (6.4km)

TIME: 2 hours

START/END: SK281722 Near the Robin Hood Inn above the A619 Chesterfield road

TERRAIN: Moderate

MAPS: OS Explorer OL 24; OS Landranger 119

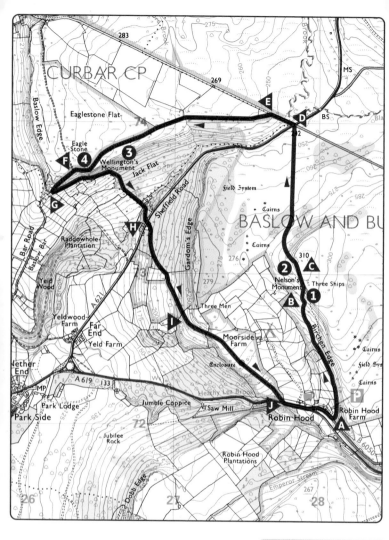

on to a turf covered moorland track.

3 Wellington Monument. The stone cross was erected in 1866. From here, there is a good view of Chatsworth House.

4 The Eagle Stone is slightly off-route but can be reached by a narrow sidepath. At one time, every young man from Baslow had to climb it before he could get married.

Birchen Edge

F Follow the moorland track as far as the moorland boundary.

G After passing the old quarry on the right, turn back left and follow the wall and fence into oak woodland. Drop downhill along a faint and windy path through trees, to a gate and a narrow path around a house.

H A horse trough to the left of Cupola Cottage marks the way. Walk steadily uphill through the scattered birch wood.

I Cross the bracken covered field.

J Climb the stone stile and turn left along the main road back to the Robin Hood Inn.

Climbers on Birchen Edge

> **This lovely walk takes in the limestone plateau with its beautiful views over the wooded valleys of Monk's, Miller's and Chee Dales**

Airy upland pastures on the limestone plateau contrast with the silvan beauty of two unspoiled dales on this walk. Monk's Dale is dry. Its river is beneath the limestone pavement but Miller's Dale has a base of impervious clay which holds the water of Derbyshire's River Wye, haunt of trout and river birds. Wormhill is a little over half way round this walk. It is the birthplace of James Brindley, builder of much of England's canal system. The quiet village makes an ideal stopping place either to explore or perhaps to buy a pot of tea. Miller's Dale station, once a busy junction where travellers to and from Buxton joined the main line to London, is now a useful car park and forms the northern end of the Monsal Trail.

The valley of the River Wye

Miller's Dale & Wormhill

Miller's Dale

Route instructions

A From Miller's Dale Station car park, walk down to the Tideswell road and turn left at the bridge. Walk with care under the double viaduct and follow the road as far as the turning opposite the Angler's Rest.

1 The twin viaducts once carried powerful steam locomotives hauling trains on a difficult section of the Midland Line along Monsal Dale. This line, from London St Pancras to Manchester Central, was originally planned to follow an easier route along the Derwent valley through Chatsworth Park to Hathersage. By 1849, when the line reached Rowsley near Matlock, the Duke of Devonshire sensed the threat to his beloved

Chatsworth and refused the railway company the right of way across his property. The railway company was forced to follow a more difficult route which climbed through Bakewell and then along the steep craggy sides of Monsal Dale.

The Midland Line closed in the 1960s and is now used as the Monsal Walking Trail between Bakewell and Miller's Dale.

B Turn left up the side road for about 150yds (135m), Then go left on a stony track behind a group of farm buildings. Join the access lane to Monksdale Farm.

2 Monksdale Farm. In the 14th century, there was a

Plan your walk

Halifax Wakefield
Rochdale Huddersfield
Oldham Barnsley
Ashton-under-Lyne
Manchester Sheffield
Stockport
Buxton Dronfield
Macclesfield Chesterfield
Congleton Matlock
Leek
Newcastle-under-Lyme Ashbourne
Stoke-on-Trent Derby
Stone Uttoxeter

DISTANCE: 5 miles (8km)

TIME: 2½ hours

START/END: SK138733 Miller's Dale station car park

TERRAIN: Moderate

MAPS:
OS Explorer OL 24;
OS Landranger 119

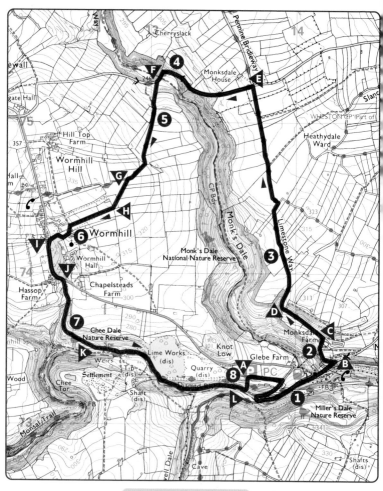

small chapel on the site of the farm – hence the name 'Monk's Dale'.

C Go through a gate on the right of the farmhouse and out onto a rough lane. Follow this towards the upland pastures.

D Follow the grassy walled lane up a steep hill at first

and then across the gentle open hill top.

3 Viewpoint. Look across the deep trough of Monk's Dale and Miller's Dale to Priestcliffe and the limestone uplands of Taddington Moor.

E Turn left, downhill along the road.

Miller's Dale & Wormhill

4 Monk's Dale Viewpoint. The special flora and fauna of this densely wooded, narrow rocky dale are protected as part of a nature reserve. Peter Dale to the right, a continuation of Monk's Dale, is not as heavily wooded and more easily accessible.

F Follow the road across the open section of Monk's Dale for about 20yds (18m) and then turn left through a narrow stone stile 100yds (92m) beyond the valley path. Climb the grassy path until it joins a narrow walled track.

5 Viewpoint. Monk's Dale is to the east, continuing northwards towards Peak Forest as a series of inter-connecting dry dales.

G Take the left fork and follow the track, later becoming a path across a series of narrow fields.

H Cross a stone stile and then walk diagonally across the long, narrow final field into Wormhill.

6 Wormhill. This quiet upland community will have changed very little since James Brindley, the canal engineer, was born here in 1716. Notice the ancient stocks to one side of the Brindley Memorial and spare a little time to look in on the 700 year old village church.

I Follow the road, to the left, downhill away from the village.

J At the bottom of the dip in the road, turn right at the signpost and go past a stone cottage, downhill through a rocky dell.

7 Viewpoint: Chee Dale Nature Reserve has ash woodland and limestone grassland. The steep sided valley of Chee Dale opposite can be seen.

K Walk down the steep scrub-covered hillside as far as the river. Do not cross but turn at the footbridge and follow the riverbank downstream under the huge, old railway bridge.

8 Viewpoint. Narrow terraces above Blackwell Dale, to the right of the main dale, mark the site of ancient fields. On the left-hand hillside are the remains of an old limestone quarry. The kilns have been preserved and can be approached by a track beyond the Miller's Dale viaduct.

L At the road bridge, turn left uphill, on the waymarked path to Miller's Dale Station.

66 There are lovely views of the surrounding moors from Solomon's Temple, a Victorian folly which sits on top of a 1,300ft (396m) prehistoric mound 99

Buxton has retained many of the attractions from its heyday as a spa town when visitors combined 'taking the waters' with an inland holiday. One of the most impressive buildings in Buxton is The Crescent built in 1780 by John Carr for the Duke of Devonshire. After an extensive restoration program it reopened in 2007 as a hotel and thermal spa.

Poole's Cavern in Buxton Country Park is open to the public and its visitor centre gives an interesting insight into the historical, geological and archaeological past. The walk skirts Grin Low Woods and then climbs out on to the stark limestone moors before moving to Solomon's Temple with its vantage point above the town.

Solomon's Temple

The Crescent, Buxton

Route instructions

1 Poole's Cavern. Classed as one of Charles Cotton's seven 'Wonders of the Peak' in 1680, this natural cave was once the home of Stone Age Man. It has attracted explorers from as far back as the 16th century – Mary Queen of Scots is said to have visited in 1582. The showcave closed in 1965 but re-opened in 1976 and its history is explained in the adjacent visitor centre.

A From Poole's Cavern car park turn right and walk back along the road towards the town.

B Follow the road past the school and round the left-hand bend. Turn right at a signposted gap between the houses and walk through a series of fields.

C Turn right along the metalled drive.

D At a group of houses, cross a cattle grid and turn right. Climb over the wall using the step stile and turn immediately left. Follow the wall uphill, keeping to the right of Fern House and its woodland. Continue ahead over the crest of the hill and down to the road.

E Bear left across the road and into the dip. Turn right through a gate on to a farm track.

F Follow the signs around the farmyard and out along its access track. Follow the

Plan your walk

DISTANCE: 4½ miles (7.2km)

TIME: 2¼ hours

START/END: SK051725 Buxton

TERRAIN: Easy; uphill sections

MAPS:
OS Explorer OL 24;
OS Landranger 119

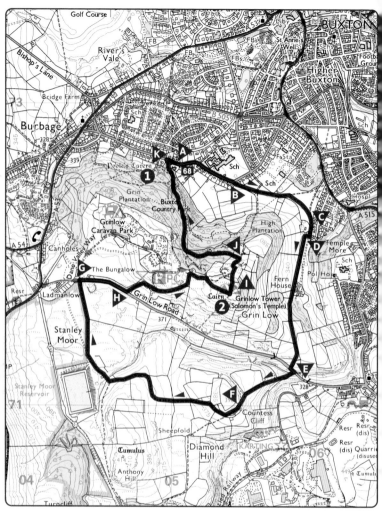

track over open fields of the limestone moor.

G Turn right and follow the road for about ¼ mile (400m).

H Turn left at a signpost, uphill along a cart track. Pass a group of farm buildings and follow the direction of a second signpost. Head towards the prominent tower on top of Grin Law.

2 Solomon's Temple. This Victorian folly built in 1895 for a local farmer and landowner, Solomon

Solomon's Temple

Mycock, by the unemployed of the area – a type of Victorian job creation scheme. It sits on top of a prehistoric mound and at 1,300ft (396m) it makes an excellent vantage point above Buxton and the surrounding moors – Mam Tor can be seen on a clear day.

▶ Go downhill through the narrow stile with a signpost and then on to a second boundary wall. Do not cross the wall.

▶ Turn left at the wall. Walk ahead on a cart track and enter the woods of Grin Plantation by climbing a gateside stile. Follow a wide path, which gradually descends beneath the mature trees. Ignore any side paths.

▶ Turn right down a flight of steps leading directly to the car park.

Solomon's Temple

> 66 This is a walk for lazy afternoons, or for an hour or so in the evening, the slight effort of climbing to the viewpoint is made worthwhile with views from the top across the Cheshire Plain to the west and Shining Tor to the east 99

People living in towns and cities surrounding the Peak District can reach its countryside in a very short period of time but none as quickly as those who live in the little industrial town of Bollington. This walk, which is a popular summer stroll for Bollington's inhabitants, starts beside the parish church and, after a short initial climb, it reaches the curious pear-shaped edifice on Kerridge Hill known as the White Nancy. The true history of the White Nancy seems to have been lost in the passage of time. We do not know who suggested its name or how its shape was decided upon. What is certain is that the local people of Bollington are very proud of this curious memorial and make sure that it is kept in good repair and given a coat of whitewash from time to time. The height is gained, it must be admitted, by some effort but, once gained, it is retained for a mile (1.6km) or so, before you return along a pleasant side valley. This is a walk for lazy summer afternoons, or for an hour or so in the evening.

White Nancy

The Cat & Fiddle

Route instructions

Plan your walk

A From Bollington's Parish Church of St. John the Baptist, follow Church Street and Lord Street uphill past the dyeworks/coating mill.

B At the bend at the top of Lord Street, go ahead through the gate and climb the steep hill towards the prominent tower of White Nancy.

1 Viewpoint. The whitewashed stone tower known as White Nancy is thought to commemorate the ending of the Napoleonic Wars. It looks to the west across the Cheshire Plain with the wooded sandstone ridge of Alderley Edge closer to hand. Eastwards, the outlook is towards Shining Tor and the Cat & Fiddle, England's second highest inn, which marks the moorland crossing of the A537.

C From White Nancy walk ahead along the crest of Kerridge Hill.

D Climb the stile on the left and walk downhill. Take the path, which slants gradually across the side of the hill, to the left of a belt of trees. Cross a wall using a stone stile. At the next wall turn left and follow the wall downhill to gain a waymarked path. Almost immediately the path divides. Bear right through the woodland.

DISTANCE: 4 miles (6.4km)

TIME: 2 hours

START/END: SJ939768 Bollington

TERRAIN: Easy; one 420ft (128m) climb

MAPS: OS Explorer OL 24; OS Landranger 118

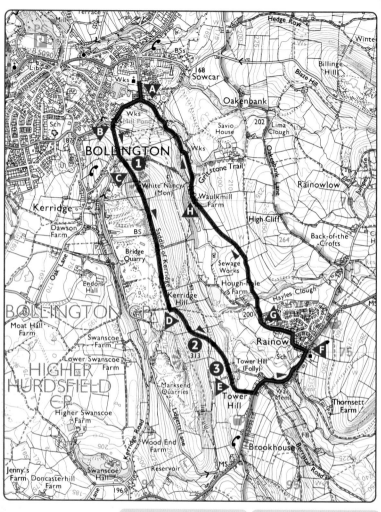

2 Viewpoint. The village of Rainow is below with the land rising towards the Cheshire Uplands. In the 18th century, the village 'mayor' was made to ride a donkey facing backwards during his inauguration ceremony.

3 Cow Lane Mill. Built in 1789 and was in use as a textile mill and later as a bleachworks until 1907. A period of excavation and conservation started in 2007 and is ongoing.

E Follow the track through the ruins of Cow Lane Mill

White Nancy

and bear left along the walled lane. Turn left at the main road.

F Turn left opposite the church. Follow Round Meadow Road, bearing left at the next junction.

G Follow the flagged path, to the right, behind a group of stone cottages, the last houses in the built up area of Rainow. Walk through a series of meadows, crossing their boundaries by stone slab squeezer stiles.

H Follow the lane between a group of cottages, then through millyards and past attractive cottages into Bollington.

View of Bollington from the White Nancy

> **"** Most visitors arriving at the lower reaches of Dovedale are content with a short stroll beyond the stepping stones at the mouth of the dale. Scenically delightful though this may be, it is only a mere hint of the attractions further upstream, which this walk helps to explore **"**

Old prints and photographs show the dale sides almost bare of trees but, in the space of a few decades, the valley became over populated by the rapid spread of ash and sycamore. In the old days, sheep and cattle were grazed within the confines of the dale which prevented the growth of intrusive saplings. Now that they no longer graze there, as a result of more intensive modern farming methods, the dale has lost this natural method of restricting the invasive spread of dense woodland. The National Trust, as owners of Dovedale, have removed much of this new growth from around special features. As a result, natural formations such as Reynard's Cave and the Twelve Apostles' Rocks, can be appreciated as they were in the past. Grass is now regenerating, holding the loose scree and the view of Dovedale is now more open. Overused footpaths have been repaired and erosion stopped and now that nature assisted by the National Trust, has taken over again, Dovedale's beauty is being preserved for the future.

Dovedale

Walkers in the valley of the River Dove, Dovedale

Route instructions

A From Dovedale car park, cross the fields behind the Izaak Walton Hotel. The path is signposted to Ilam.

B Do not cross the road but turn sharp right at a signpost and follow the grassy path beneath Bunster Hill. As the angle increases, zigzagging will make the climb that much easier.

1 St Bertram's Well. St Bertram or Bertelin brought Christianity to Dovedale in the 7th or 8th century. Legend tells us that he became a hermit following the death of his Irish born wife and his only child who were attacked by a pack of wolves nearby. Heartbroken, he spent the rest of his life in this remote hollow.

C At the top of the slope, cross the stile and follow a pathless course across the next field. Aim for the barn on the crest of the rise.

2 Viewpoint. The mock tudor chimneys of Victorian Ilam Hall can be seen in the valley bottom. Beyond the hall, Hinckley Wood shrouds the steep sides of the lower Manifold Valley.

D Go right, then left through two field gates at the side of a stone barn. Follow the track on the right of the shelter belt of trees. Turn right to reach Air Cottage.

3 Viewpoint. Air Cottage must have one of the finest views in the Peak District.

Plan your walk

DISTANCE: 4½ miles (7.2km)

TIME: 2¼ hours

START/END: SK146508 Dovedale car park

TERRAIN: Moderate; one 538ft (164m) climb

MAPS:
OS Explorer OL 24;
OS Landranger 119

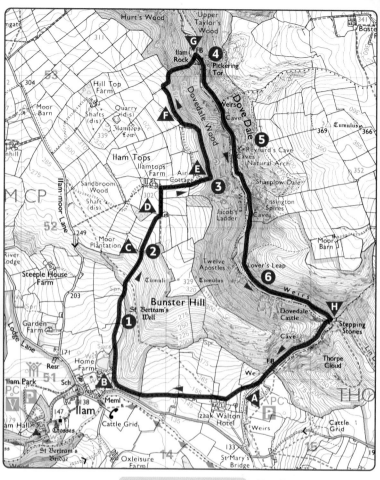

Set high above Dovedale, you can see Thorpe Cloud on the right, then Lover's Leap, Tissington Spires and Reynard's Cave. The middle and upper dale can be seen curving away to the north as a narrow ravine cleaving its way through the limestone uplands.

E Turn right through a gate at the start of the cottage drive. Follow the waymarked path around to the left and along the valley side above the trees. Head for a gate to the right of the farm track.

F Go through the gate and follow the path along the edge of the woodland. Stay on the path as it turns right and drops down the steep valley side using occasional wooden steps, which

Dovedale

eventually reaches the riverside.

G Turn right at the path junction at the side of the River Dove. Cross sides by the footbridge below Ilam Rock and follow the riverside path downstream.

4 Lion Rock at the foot of Pickering Tor is aptly named. Look back upstream for the best view.

5 Reynard's Cave. Look out for a natural arch high above the path on the left. A cave beyond the arch was used as a hiding place during troubled times following the end of the Roman occupation. Arrow heads and pottery have been found in its recesses.

6 Lover's Leap. The path climbs above the river by a series of steps to reach this rocky vantage point. Opposite, there are rocky spires known as the Twelve Apostles. Autumn is the best time for this part of the dale because this is when the trees are most colourful. There is no record of any star-crossed lovers jumping from this point but there is a cautionary tale concerning the Irish Dean of Clogher. In 1761 he tried to ride over the rock carrying a young lady companion as a pillion passenger. The horse stumbled on the slippery rocks and all three fell towards the river. The Dean was killed and is buried at Ashbourne. The lady was more fortunate, however, as she was saved by her long hair which caught in the branches of a tree.

H Cross the Dovedale stepping stones and turn left along the metalled road back to the car park. If the river is in flood and the stepping stones are under water, follow the left bank of the river and cross lower down at the footbridge about 150yds (164m) from the car park.

Thorpe Cloud, Dovedale

❝ This 4 mile (6.4km) walk gives you lovely views over the River Dove which has cut a steep-sided valley through the limestone ❞

From the village of Longnor, we visit two major Peakland valleys. At first, the underlying strata is shale and the River Manifold flows in a broad fertile trough. Across Sheen Moor, the River Dove has carved a steep sided valley through its limestone bedrock.

Longnor Two Valleys Walk

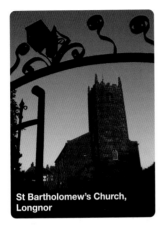

St Bartholomew's Church, Longnor

Route instructions

1 Longnor. There is no longer a market but a renovated plaque above the market hall has a list of the tolls due to the Harpur-Crewe estate.

A Follow the road east from Longnor for about 150yds (140m). Turn right along the signposted lane to Folds End Farm. Go left through the farmyard. Climb over a stone stile and turn half-right to follow a field path to the River Manifold.

B Turn left along the gravel surfaced farm track. Keep left through the farmyard and then right on a concrete track. Through the gate it becomes a rough track. Follow the track uphill as far as the road.

2 Viewpoint. Longnor village is above the Manifold valley. The grassy shoulder beyond Longnor marks the boundary between gritstone and shales of the Western Part and the Dovedale limestone.

C Turn right along the road for about 500yds (460m), Climb the stone stile and turn left across three fields. Turn right, down the track to Under Whittle Farm.

3 View of the Upper Dove. Grassy mounds in the valley bottom mark the motte and bailey of Pilsbury Castle.

D Climb the stile at the top of the farm garden. Follow a waymarked path. Turn right onto a private lane. After

Plan your walk

DISTANCE: 4 miles (6.4km)

TIME: 2 hours

START/END: SK088649 Longnor

TERRAIN: Moderate

MAPS:
OS Explorer OL 24;
OS Landranger 119

Halifax   Wakefield
Rochdale   Huddersfield
Oldham   Barnsley
Ashton-under-Lyne
Manchester   Sheffield
Stockport
Buxton   Dronfield
Macclesfield   Chesterfield
Congleton   Matlock
Leek
Newcastle-under-Lyme   Ashbourne
Stoke-on-Trent   Derby
Stone   Uttoxeter

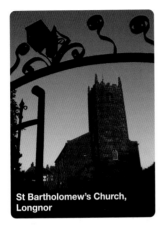

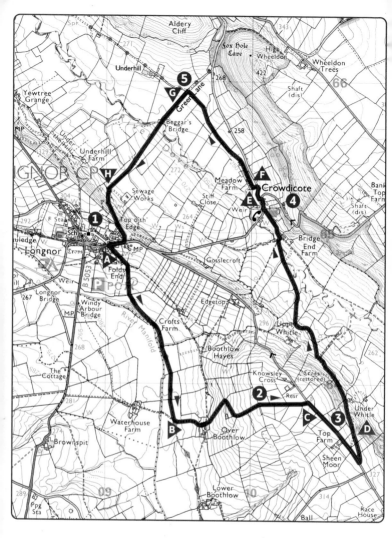

about 200yds (185m) pick up the waymarked path again on the left. Pass a pair of barns and, following waymarks and stiles, cross a series of fields to the River Dove. Walk upstream.

E Cross the river by the footbridge. Follow the track beyond it as far as the lane and turn left into Crowdicote. Go right on the main road, then left along a side lane.

Longnor Two Valleys Walk

4 Crowdicote. The village is named after Saxon Cruda who built the first farm on this spot. The Pack Horse Inn is a welcome sight on a hot day.

F Leave the side road. Follow the signpost along a lane to open fields.

5 View of the upper Dove and the reef knoll hills of its eastern flank.

G Go left along the wide grassy river access track. Cross the footbridge, then climb a low rise to reach a shallow side valley.

H Turn left at a stone barn and climb along a gravel lane to Longnor.

Manifold Valley

> 66 Starting in the village of Elton, once a centre of lead mining, the route takes you past Robin Hood's Stride, where there are the remains of a stone circle, and on to a hermit's cave beneath Cratcliffe Rocks 99

The walk starts in Elton where the friendly cottages were once the homes of lead miners. On the surrounding upland, the route passes several pre-Christian remains and a hermit's cave.

Elton & Robin Hood's Stride

Halifax · Wakefield
Rochdale
Huddersfield
Oldham · Barnsley
Ashton-under-Lyne
Manchester
Stockport · Sheffield
Buxton · Dronfield · Chesterfield
Macclesfield
Congleton · Matlock
Leek
Newcastle-under-Lyme · Ashbourne
Stoke-on-Trent
· Derby
· Stone · Uttoxeter

DISTANCE: 3 miles (4.8km)

TIME: 1½ hours

START/END: SK222610 Elton

TERRAIN: Easy / Moderate

MAPS:
OS Explorer OL 24;
OS Landranger 119

Route instructions

1 Elton is a village which once made its living from lead mining. In fact, there was a mine next to the church – you can see where it was from the rough ground next to the church yard. The font inside the church has an unusual history. When the church was rebuilt in Victorian times, the original font found its way to Youlgreave and Elton had to make do with a copy.

A Turn right by the church at the end of Elton's main street. Fork left at the Old Rectory and go through a gate. Follow the field path across the valley.

B Cross the minor road, go through a stone squeezer

stile opposite and follow a field path.

C Cross the access lane and keep to the left of a prominent knoll. Skirt Tomlinson Wood by following its boundary wall to the left and then a line of telegraph poles.

2 Viewpoint. Youlgreave sits astride its ridge above Bradford Dale.

D Bear left at a rough cart track and, a little later, right over a ditch marked by a signpost and gate. Go to the left up the field and over a stile into mixed woodland.

E Follow the woodland track as far as the road.

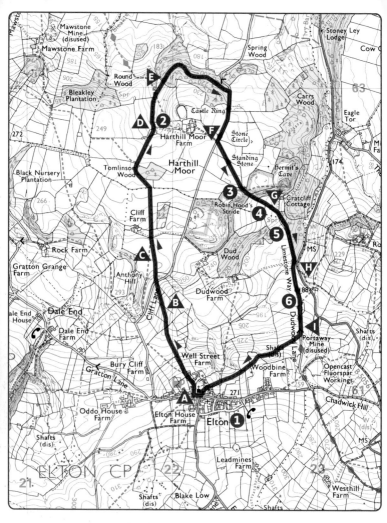

Turn right, uphill along the road and then left on a signposted field path. Aim towards the prominent rocks of Robin Hood's Stride.

3 Viewpoint. Robin Hood's Stride dominates the skyline in front. To the left in the corner of a field, stand four enigmatic stones, remains of a circle of nine.

Immediately left of Robin Hood's Stride, follow a side path through bracken and pine wood to the foot of

Elton & Robin Hood's Stride

Cratcliffe Rocks. Return to the main path to continue the walk.

4 There is a hermit's cave beneath Cratcliffe Rocks. It is not known who the hermit was but there is a record in the archives of Haddon Hall showing a payment to 'Ye harmytt' for the supply of ten rabbits in 1549.

5 The walk follows part of an ancient Portway.

▶ Do not go as far as the main road but walk ahead up the narrower side road.

6 Viewpoint. Vagrants once mistook Robin Hood's Stride for a Manor House and visited it in the hope of receiving charity.

▶ Turn right at a signpost and cross the sparsely wooded slope. Go through the gate on the left just after the sports field and follow the track across to Elton.

Limestone Way

> **Between March and October you can take the cable car up to the Heights of Abraham if you wish to avoid walking up the steep path to this vantage point**

Matlock developed as a spa town during the Victorian era with an enthusiasm which culminated in the construction of the massive Smedley Hydro dominating the northern hillside above the town. The building is now used as the offices of Derbyshire Council. Thermal water, still flows but, apart from its use in the indoor swimming pool of the New Bath Hotel, it is largely ignored.

The Victorians fancifully compared the local landscape to Switzerland and this walk certainly has an alpine flavour. There is a cable car system from the foot of High Tor to the summit of the Heights of Abraham (the cable car is closed Nov–Feb). The latter is an attractive area of landscaped woodland high above the Derwent Valley.

Small fees are payable to enter High Tor with its roofless caverns and woodland walks. A fee is also charged for entry to the Heights of Abraham. This covers show caves, other amenities and the cable car. From the Heights of Abraham, the walk follows a miners' path to Bonsall and its unique market cross. The route returns to Matlock by way of airy Masson Hill.

High Tor & the Heights of Abraham

Matlock Bath

Route instructions

A From Matlock, follow the riverside path through Hall Leys Park. Go under the railway bridge as far as a footbridge. Do not cross, but turn left up a narrow lane.

B Turn right through a gate into the grounds of High Tor. A grassy path leads to the summit café.

1 Viewpoint. The River Derwent has carved a narrow gorge at the foot of the sheer limestone cliff of High Tor. On the opposite side of the valley, the wooded slopes of the Heights of Abraham lead to Masson Hill. Turn about and allow your eyes to follow the downward slope of High Tor. The hill which rises beyond is composed of

gritstone lying on top of the limestone of High Tor. This is Riber Hill, dominated by a curious folly known as Riber Castle. Built in the mid 1800s by John Smedley as a hydropathic hotel, it never flourished, mainly because there was a poor water supply and it fell into disuse in the 1940s. It later became a wildlife park which subsequently closed in 2000.

The summit of High Tor has a series of deep roofless caverns which can be explored without a torch.

C There are at least three alternative paths from High Tor, including one which follows a narrow ledge across the upper face.

Plan your walk

DISTANCE: 4½ miles (7.2km)

TIME: 2¼ hours

START/END: SK298602 Matlock

TERRAIN: Easy

MAPS:
OS Explorer OL 24;
OS Landranger 119

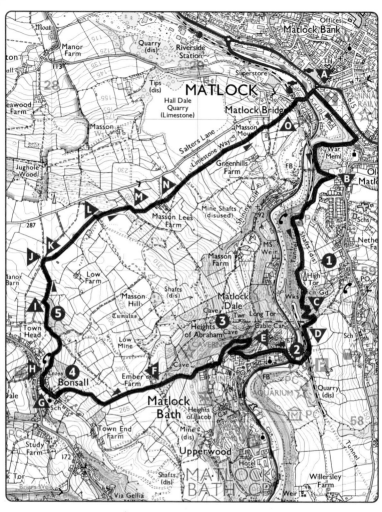

D Take the cable car to the Heights of Abraham. ***Note that the cable car is closed Nov-Feb.*** If closed, follow the station approach to cross the A6 and climb Holme Road to Upperwood Road. Follow Upperwood Road as far as the lower entrance to the woodlands.

Continue for 110yds (100m) and follow a steep path on the right up the hillside.

2 If following the alternative route, Matlock Bath's 'Swiss style' station is very much in keeping with the alpine flavour of this walk.

High Tor & the Heights of Abraham

E Follow the gravel track for about 40yds (37m) beyond the upper cable car station and turn left along a level woodland path at the boundary of the gardens.

3 The Heights of Abraham. This is a convenient refreshment stop. The name commemorates General Wolfe's battle with the French in 1759 to gain control of Canada. The Great Rutland Cavern is nearby. Here you can experience the sights and sounds of a working Derbyshire lead mine in the 17th century. The Victoria Tower is a few yards from the upper cable station and was built as part of a 19th century 'job creation scheme'. The tower is a good vantage point for viewing the surrounding scenery.

F At a complex track junction by Ember Farm, bear right towards the farm, then left away from it, along the walled access lane and walk down to Bonsall village.

G Turn right at the church and follow the road as far as the market cross. The seventeenth century Kings Head pub is opposite.

4 The pillar of the market cross is mounted on a steep conical plinth which has 10 steps on its uphill side and 13 downhill.

H Follow the walled lane up a steep hill, to the right of the cross. Keep left at the end of the surfaced section to walk along a tree-shaded path.

5 View of Bonsall village tucked in its hillside cleft.

I Turn right at a T junction. Go through a field gate to follow a hedge and trees.

J At the gate go through a gap in the right hand hedge and wall. Cross a small field keeping between two barns.

K Go through a squeezer stile into the narrow field.

L Cross the gravel lane and pass through the gap in the wall on its opposite side. Go down the grassy hillside on a faint path.

M Keeping to the right of a boundary hedge, walk downhill through two fields towards the left hand side of Masson Lees Farm.

N Cross the lane and enter the lower field through an old iron gateway, Follow the hedge and cross field boundaries by stone and wooden stiles.

O Go through a stile at the bottom of the steep field. Climb down the steps at the side of the large house and join the road into Matlock.

66 This walk is particularly enjoyable for those with an interest in industrial heritage as you will see old canals, railway routes with winding houses and workshops, quarries and a museum in Arkwright's 1771 water-powered cotton mill **99**

Richard Arkwright came to Cromford in 1771 and built a cotton mill using the Derwent to power his newly invented spinning frames, completely revolutionising the textile industry. Part of his original mill is now a museum. Beyond it is the tow path of a preserved canal – the one time commercial lifeline of Cromford. The towpath leads to the foot of Sheep Pasture, better known as the High Peak Incline. The stark outcrop of Black Rocks marks the end of the climb and a track which was old long before Arkwright came to Cromford.

Cromford & the High Peak Incline

Cromford Canal

Route instructions

A Follow the towpath from Cromford Wharf away from the car park.

1 The canal, built in 1793, gave Arkwright's mills a link with the developing Midlands. It ran for 14½ miles (23km) from Cromford to the Erewash Canal and included four tunnels and 14 locks. The 6 mile (9.7km) long section between Cromford and Ambergate is a Site of Special Scientific Interest.

B Cross the canal at the swing bridge and go to the right behind a low brick building. Climb the High Peak Incline. The climb is steep but trees offer plenty of shade on a hot day.

2 High Peak Junction. The junction is between railway and canal. Here, there are the oldest railway workshops in the world and a visitor centre.

3 Sheep Pasture Incline. A plaque on the wall of the repair shop at the foot of the incline briefly explains the history of the 33 mile (53m) High Peak Railway. The line was opened in 1831 and was introduced as a means of connecting two canals – the Cromford and the High Peak, near Whaley Bridge. It was impossible to build a canal across the waterless limestone uplands but the railway was designed as though it was a canal. Rather than go round or through hills, the line

Plan your walk

DISTANCE: 3½ miles (5.6km)

TIME: 1¾ hours

START/END: SK301571 Cromford northern car park on edge of the village

TERRAIN: Easy; one 530ft (162m) climb

MAPS: OS Explorer OL 24; OS Landranger 119

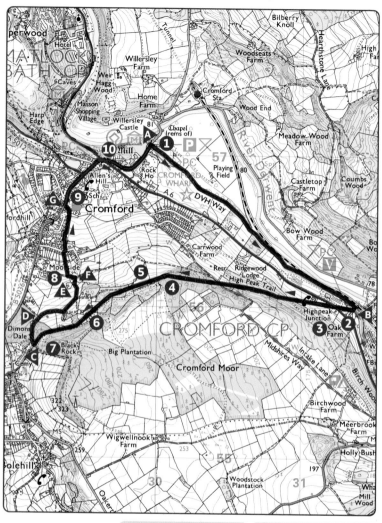

climbs in a series of steep inclines, with motive power supplied by stationary winding engines on the steepest sections. The line climbed to Parsley Hay and went on to Hindlow, above Buxton, before dropping into the Goyt Valley and Whaley Bridge by a further three inclines. As an indication of the canal mentality, stations along the High Peak were always known as 'wharfs'.

4 Sheep Pasture Winding House. The tall building on

Cromford & the High Peak Incline

the left of the track housed a steam-powered winding engine to haul wagons up the incline.

5 Viewpoint looking north along the Derwent Gorge. Cromford is below and you can see Willersley Castle in its parkland. The A6 cuts through the rocks of much widened Scarthin Nick. Looking upstream, Matlock Bath surmounted by the wooded Heights of Abraham and the bare limestone face of High Tor opposite, carry the eye towards Matlock Moor.

6 Viewpoint. Dene Quarry is opposite. Massive steps or 'benches' are cutting deep into the limestone hillside and gradually eating away Cromford Hill.

7 Black Rocks. There was once an extensive lead mine beneath this point which is now marked by the overgrown spoil heaps and ruined buildings. A forest trail over the top of Black Rocks starts at this point.

C Go right, through a gate at the side of the High Peak Trail. Walk downhill on a winding path through the tree-covered spoil heaps.

D Turn right in the clearing at the bottom of the wooded slope. Climb to the boundary wall and cross by

a gap in the wall. Follow a field path, keeping to the left of the house.

E Go through a narrow gate and head left, downhill along an access lane.

F Leave the lane by going through a squeezer stile on the right. Follow the narrow hedge-lined path down to the outer limits of Cromford.

8 The lane is called Bedehouse Lane, an ancient way between Wirksworth and Cromford.

G At the road, turn right down Cromford Hill and walk through the village. Cross the main A6 and follow the side road past Arkwright's Mill as far as the canal car park.

9 North Street. The third storeys of the well-preserved cottages once accommodated handloom weavers' lofts.

10 Cromford Mill. Richard Arkwright established the first successful water powered cotton mill on this site in 1771. The Arkwright Society has established a museum inside part of Cromford Mill which is dedicated to the father of the factory system. The mill is now part of the Derwent Valley World Heritage site.

> **"** For part of this walk you are following the Tissington Trail. This was one of the first in the country to use old railway tracks and follows the Ashbourne-Buxton line **"**

The two villages visited on this walk, on either side of the Bletch Brook, are built on ancient foundations. The houses of Tissington are grouped around the ancestral home of the Fitzherberts. Villagers decorate Tissington's five wells with floral pictures every Ascension Day as an ancient tribute to their pure water. Parwich is equally attractive in its own way but not as well known and, for some people, this could be an attraction in itself.

View from the Tissington Trail

Tissington & Parwich

Tissington Hall

Route instructions

A From Tissington Trail car park, go left through the village, then right past the hall. Turn right again at the far end of the village.

1 Tissington. The hall was built in the early 17th century and the church is even older. When they dress the village wells, it is said they are remembering that the Black Death never reached here.

B Turn left by the last cottage and follow a signposted and waymarked path across a series of fields, crossing walls by stiles or gates.

2 Low ridges are the remains of mediaeval field systems.

C Keep to the right of Crakelow Farm and cross the bridge over the Tissington Trail. Keep right and walk downhill by a pathless route across four fields, to the right of an old barn.

D Cross Bletch Brook and climb the hillside by following a boundary hedge. Cross two other field boundaries.

E Walk along the sunken track.

F Go through a squeezer stile, away from the track and over a field. Aim to the right of a ruined barn. Climb a stile in the hedge and walk downhill.

Plan your walk

DISTANCE: 3¾ miles (6km)

TIME: 2 hours

START/END: SK178521 Tissington

TERRAIN: Easy

MAPS: OS Explorer OL 24; OS Landranger 119

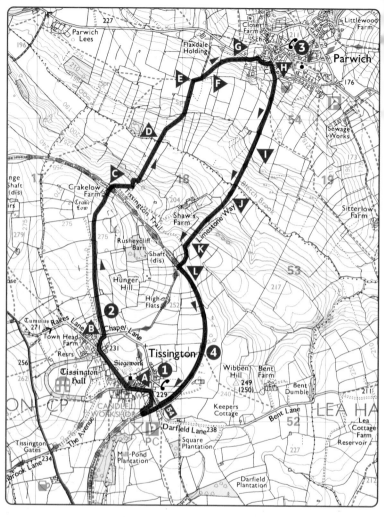

G At the bottom corner of the field, go through two gates and join the road. Turn right into Parwich.

3 Parwich village has a delightful church. There is one remaining pub close to the church.

H Walk through the village, past the cave on the right and go through an awkward squeezer stile by the side of a farm house.

I Follow the hedge to the final slopes down to the

Tissington & Parwich

Bletch Brook. Cross the brook by its footbridge.

J ▶ Climb uphill as indicated by the signpost and cross stiles.

K ▶ Go left along the farm lane as far as the railway bridge.

L ▶ Immediately after the bridge, go through a gate on the left and walk down to the trail. Follow the trail straight on and walk for about ¾ mile (1.2km) back to the car park.

④ Tissington Trail. The trail, which was one of the first in the country to use old railway tracks, follows the Ashbourne-Buxton line to its junction with the High Peak trail near Parsley Hey.

Tissington Trail

> **This gentle walk begins by a riverside terrace where 17th century dramatist William Congreve wrote part of his comedy 'The Old Bachelor' and climbs up above Hinkley Woods where, according to the season, you will see anemones, celandines, bluebells and primroses**

Tucked away on a bend of the Manifold river, Ilam village was built in the 1830s on the instructions of Jesse Watts Russell. The original Victorian houses of the village echo the fairytale image of the hall, built at a time when skilful labour was cheap. It was also a time when people could be moved at the whim of their landlords if, as in this case, he wanted more space or privacy.

The Ilam Hall we see today, with its Tudor style chimneys and mock Gothic architecture, is only part of the original building. The central tower and most of the formal rooms were demolished in the early 1930s. The rest of the building was about to suffer the same fate when it was bought by Sir Robert McDougall, a Manchester businessman. He had the remaining parts of the hall made habitable and presented it, together with the grounds, to the National Trust. Ilam Hall is now a youth hostel.

Ilam Hall and village replaced dwellings of a much earlier vintage. The shaft of a stone cross was found in the foundations of a cottage during the rebuilding of the village. It now stands to one side of the riverside walk and is thought to date from around 1050, commemorating a battle between local Saxons and invading Danes.

Ilam Hall

Ilam Hall

Route instructions

A From the car park in the grounds of Ilam Hall, go past the National Trust Visitor Centre and follow the path down steps to the riverside.

1 St Bertram lived as a hermit in the small cave above the point where water bubbles out beneath a rocky overhang at the side of the path. The water has travelled for about 5 miles (8km) underground from Darfur Bridge near Wetton (see Walk 20) emerging at this point. In spring, the woods are full of anemones and celandines, then later primroses and bluebells compete for the sunlight as the trees come into leaf. Nature later creates its masterwork of subtle browns, reds and yellows as the beech leaves die every autumn.

2 Battle Cross. Found when Watts-Russell rebuilt the village.

B Turn left over the second footbridge Ignore the main path on the right beyond the bridge but follow a pathless course uphill towards the wooded skyline. Use a stone stile in a ruined wall as a route marker.

3 Viewpoint. Ilam Hall can be glimpsed through the trees and beyond it rise Bunster Hill and Thorpe Cloud at the southern entrance to Dovedale.

Plan your walk

DISTANCE: 4½ miles (7.2km)

TIME: 2¼ hours

START/END: SK131508 Car park in the grounds of Ilam Hall

TERRAIN: Easy

MAPS:
OS Explorer 259;
OS Landranger 119

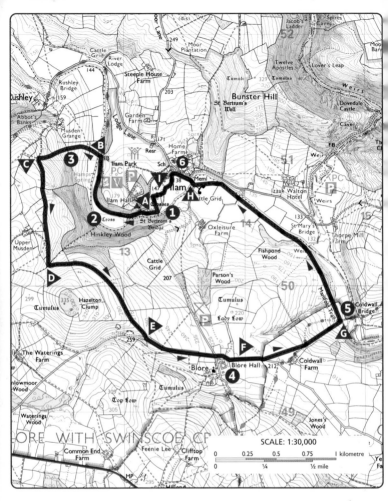

C Turn left on a grassy track and follow the boundary wall.

D Cross the dry valley and aim for the broad track which curves uphill around wooded Hazelton Clump.

E Climb a stile and turn left along the metalled road.

Follow it over Blore cross-roads to Coldwall Farm.

4 The 16th century farmhouse, which is set back from the road, was formerly Blore Hall.

F Turn left away from the road, go through the farmyard and into the field.

Ilam Hall

Walk downhill, tracing the line of the abandoned turnpike road.

▶ Keeping to the west bank (Blore side) of the river, turn left away from the bridge and walk upstream. Follow a fence above the hawthorn-covered slopes until a gap gives access to the riverbank.

⑤ Coldwall Bridge. Sturdy buttresses show how this bridge over the Dove has outlasted its need.

▶ Climb the short flight of steps to the bridge and turn right, along the road into Illam village.

⑥ Ilam village. The elaborate Gothic cross is a memorial to Mrs Watts-Russell, a constant reminder to the villagers of this not over popular lady.

▶ Turn left past Dovedale House along the church path to return to Ilam Hall and its car park. There is a National Trust shop and café in the grounds.

Ilam village

❝ An easy walk starting in the village of Flash, once the haunt of counterfeiters, taking in views towards the dramatic outlines of the Ramshaw Rocks and the uppermost boulders of the Roaches **❞**

Flash is the highest village in England, a place where winter starts early and lingers long after spring has arrived in more sheltered places. The wind is keen but refreshing and the views are far ranging. Counterfeiters once carried out their illicit trade in remote farmhouses around Flash and its name has since become linked with any suspicious or 'flashy' object.

Three Shires Head

The Roaches

Route instructions

A Walk out of Flash village along the minor road to the right of the New Inn.

B At the bend at the bottom of the hill, turn right along the concrete drive. Do not enter the farmyard.

C Turn left across the wooden footbridge and follow the direction of the signpost to Three Shires Head. Climb slightly and cross a couple of fields. Turn right at the farm buildings to reach the lane.

D Go left along the lane, which is metalled at first but later becomes a sandy, almost level track into the Dane Valley.

1 Viewpoint looking south towards the dramatic outlines of Ramshaw Rocks. The uppermost boulders of the Roaches can also be seen, above the heather moors.

E Go through the gate to the right of Three Shires Bridge and climb the stony track.

2 Three Shires Head. The bridge which marks the junction of the counties of Cheshire, Staffordshire and Derbyshire once carried trains of packhorses and travellers on their journeys between Cheshire, The Potteries and South Yorkshire. Panniers' Pool, beneath the bridge, probably got its name as

Plan your walk

DISTANCE: 4 miles (6.4km)

TIME: 2 hours

START/END: SK025672 Flash

TERRAIN: Easy

MAPS: OS Explorer OL 24; OS Landranger 119

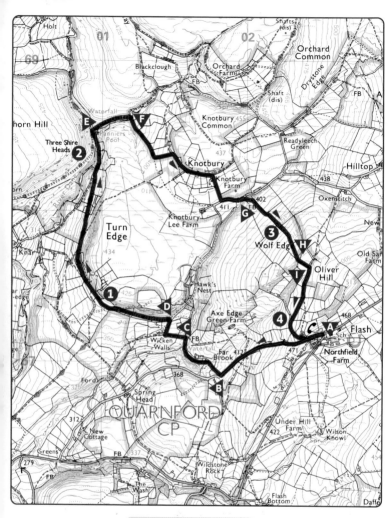

the resting and watering place for the pack animals.

F Turn right over a single-arched bridge. Follow the walled track to the road and continue along it.

G Turn right, over the stone clapper bridge.

Follow the direction indicated by a white waymark arrow on a black disc, which points uphill to the heather moor. The path is indistinct in places but follows a wire fence on top of an old bilberry covered wall. Change sides as indicated by stiles.

Three Shires Head

3 Viewpoint. Shutlingsloe peeps invitingly over the moorland ridge opposite. Tiny farmsteads dot the valley sides. The land is poor and many farms are no longer able to support full time agriculture. Most are now run as part-time farms or even as second homes.

▶ Go diagonally across the rocky crest of the moor.

▶ Turn right along the rough moorland path and join a walled track which runs downhill into Flash.

4 Viewpoint looking down the Dane Valley.

Three Shires Head

❝ Following the lovely River Dove downstream from Viator's Bridge the walk arrives at Dove Holes, these are curious, rounded, water-worn holes in the limestone about 20ft (6m) deep **❞**

It is over 300 years since Izaak Walton fished in the River Dove with his impecunious friend, Charles Cotton of Beresford Hall. Apart from some modern traffic on the short stretch of road through Milldale, Dovedale and its famous trout stream have changed little since Walton and Cotton spent time on its banks, angling and philosophising. Walton referred to the Dove as being 'The finest river that I ever saw and the fullest of fish'. A sentiment true even today. The route of the walk follows the river downstream from Viator's Bridge as far as the curious rock formation known as Dove Holes. A secluded dry dale on the left leads to Hanson Grange Farm before joining an ancient packhorse way back to Milldale.

Viator's Bridge, Milldale

Viator's Bridge

Plan your walk

DISTANCE: 2¼ miles (3.6km)

TIME: 1¼ hours

START/END: SK137548 Milldale

TERRAIN: Easy

MAPS:
OS Explorer OL 24;
OS Landranger 119

Route instructions

A Park about 300yds (275m) west of Milldale and walk downstream from Viator's Bridge using the riverside path.

1 The thin alkaline soil on the craggy valley sides, supports many semi-alpine plants such as thyme and dwarf cranesbill. Rock outcrops on the opposite bank are used by local rock climbers.

B Turn left below Dove Holes and follow the direction of the finger post indicating Alsop le Dale. Climb the tree-lined dry dale.

2 Dove Holes. These massive water-worn holes appear, at first glance, to be the start of an extensive cave system but are, in fact, only 20 ft (6m) deep. This is a good vantage point from which to view the dale.

3 The Nabs. These are the rocky crags guarding the exit fom this dry dale.

C Turn left through a stile at the dale head and follow a series of stiles to the right of Hanson Grange Farm. Join its exit lane about 100yds (91m) beyond the farm.

4 Hanson Grange. There were several extensive monastic sheep walks in the area until the Dissolution. Hanson Grange was part of one. The farm house looks Jacobean but is probably built on older foundations.

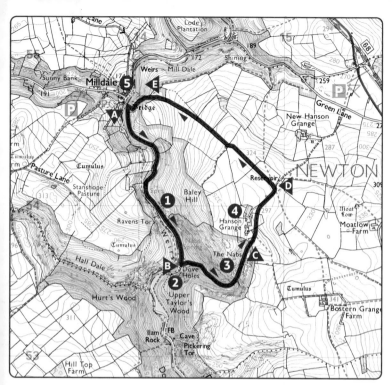

Dove Holes

Viator's Bridge, Milldale

Dovedale near Milldale

D At the end of the partly walled section of the farm lane, turn left as indicated by the signpost. Follow its direction across a series of fields, towards Milldale.

E Zigzag downhill on an ancient packhorse way into Milldale.

5 Milldale. The Dove is crossed by the narrow packhorse bridge known as Viator's Bridge. The bridge earned its name from a reference in Izaak Walton's famous treatise, 'The Compleat Angler'. He referred to himself as Viator (The Traveller) and Cotton as Piscator (The Angler). To the left of the bridge stands part of Ochre Mill. It was powered by water which ran along the leat on the west side of the river below Shining Tor. Upstream was Lode Mill and the two mills gave Milldale its name.

"Part of this walk follows the River Manifold and takes the route of the Manifold Valley Light Railway, a narrow gauge line which ran between 1904 and 1934 and was mainly used to transport milk from the dairies in the region"

Starting at Wetton, an airy upland village, the walk crosses broad pastures before climbing down through an ancient coral reef into the Manifold Valley. A disused mill at this point is now a welcoming café, well placed for a pause before the steep, climb to mysterious Thor's Cave.

Thor's Cave

The Manifold Trail

Route instructions

A Park in Wetton and follow the village street past the church. Where the road turns left, follow the direction of the signpost to 'Back of Ecton'.

B Go through the gate and stone squeezer stile on either side of the small, disused quarry. Follow a faint field path as far as the field boundary below Wetton Hill.

1 Viewpoint. Butterton church spire rises above the Manifold Valley.

C Bear right, away from the wall.

D Go over the stile in the corner of the field and climb the next to its top boundary.

Climb the stile, turn right and follow the path to the road, Follow the road back left up the hill for about 75yds (70m).

E Turn right, along an access drive and left at its junction with another track.

F Where the farm track turns right, go left following the boundary wall downhill. Move over to the right and then back left through the opening in the fence. Turn right through a stone squeezer stile, then follow the path down into the dry valley.

2 The prominent knoll to the left of the path is aptly called the Sugarloaf.

Plan your walk

DISTANCE: 4 miles (6.4km)

TIME: 2 hours

START/END: SK109551 Wetton

TERRAIN: Moderate; one climb of 295ft (90m)

MAPS: OS Explorer OL 24; OS Landranger 119

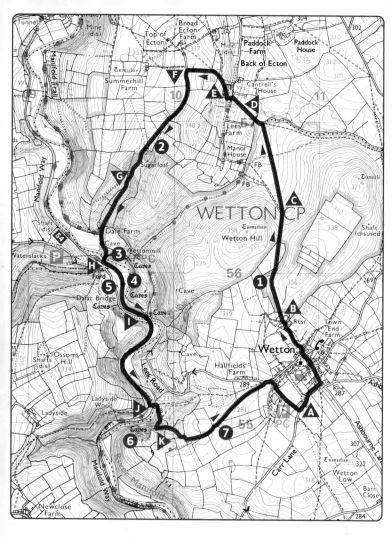

G Continue down the dry valley through the stockyard at Dale Farm and into the Manifold Valley.

3 Wettonmill. Once ground flour for the surrounding villages.

H Turn left along the valley road, then right and left over the river.

4 The valley section of this walk follows part of the route of the Manifold Valley Light Railway, a narrow

Thor's Cave

gauge line which ran between Hulme End and Waterhouses from 1904 to 1934.

5 Dafar Bridge. In dry weather, the River Manifold disappears underground at this point, reappearing near Ilam Hall.

▶ Go through a gate, away from the road, along the old railway track.

▶ Turn left over a footbridge and follow the stepped path uphill. After about 330yds (300m) turn right and follow steps back up to Thor's Cave.

6 Thor's Cave makes a perfect frame for a breathtaking view of the Manifold Valley.

K▶ From the front of the cave, follow the concessionary path and walled lane to Wetton.

7 Viewpoint. The slender spire of Grindon church stands out across the Manifold.

Manifold Valley

Photo credits

Page 4: © David Hughes / Shutterstock
Page 5: © David Hughes / Shutterstock
Page 8: © Mark William Richardson / Shutterstock
Page 12: © Richard Bowden / Shutterstock
© David Hughes / Shutterstock
Page 16: © Duncan Payne / Shutterstock
Page 17: © Duncan Payne / Shutterstock
Page 18: © Duncan Payne / Shutterstock
Page 19: © Stephen Meese / Shutterstock
Page 20: © David Hughes / Shutterstock
Page 21: © bouldie / Flickr
Page 23: © Half a world away / Flickr
Page 24: © David Hughes / Shutterstock
Page 25: © Smabs Sputzer / Flickr
Page 27: © MGSpiller / Flickr
Page 28: © David Hughes / Shutterstock
Page 29: © Jane McIlroy / Shutterstock
Page 31: © Rich B-S / Flickr
Page 32: © Chris Loneragan / Shutterstock
Page 33: © g-hat / Flickr
Page 35: © Polandeze / Flickr
Page 36: © Richard Pigott / Shutterstock
Page 37: © g-hat / Flickr
Page 39: © Sheffield Tiger / Flickr
Page 40: © Richard Williamson / Shutterstock
Page 41: © Mikey Bean / Flickr
Page 43: © Mikey Bean / Flickr
Page 44: © David Hughes / Shutterstock
Page 45: © Robbo-Man / Flickr
Page 48: © Frankie Roberto / Flickr
Page 49: © Parkie / Flickr

Page 51: © Frankie Roberto / Flickr
Page 52: © Stanth / Shutterstock
Page 53: © Haversack / Flickr
Page 55: © Smabs Sputzer / Flickr
Page 56: © David Hughes / Shutterstock
Page 57: © David Hughes / Shutterstock
Page 59: © David Hughes / Shutterstock
Page 60: © David Hughes / Shutterstock
Page 61: © bouldie / Flickr
Page 63: © David Hughes / Shutterstock
Page 64: © Robert Morris / Alamy
Page 65: © David Hughes / Shutterstock
Page 67: © Darren Copley / Flickr
Page 68: © Sonia Dawkins
Page 69: © Swimboy1 / Flickr
Page 72: © David Hughes / Shutterstock
Page 73: © Jonathan Gill / Flickr
Page 76: © David Hughes / Shutterstock
Page 77: © David Hughes / Shutterstock
Page 79: © David Hughes / Shutterstock
Page 80: © David Hughes / Shutterstock
Page 81: © bouldie / Flickr
Page 83: © David Hughes / Shutterstock
Page 84: © Smabs Sputzer / Flickr
Page 85: © xJasonRogersx / Flickr
Page 87: © Tony Comerford / Flickr
Page 88: © Sonia Dawkins
Page 89: © Andreadg / Flickr
Page 90: © Andreadg / Flickr
Page 91: © Andreadg / Flickr
Page 92: © David Hughes / Shutterstock
Page 93: © David Hughes / Shutterstock
Page 95: © Magic Foundry / Flickr